How to handle Conflicts and Collective Bargaining?

By

Chakrapani Srinivasa

How to handle Conflicts and Collective Bargaining?

By

Chakrapani Srinivasa

Chakrapani Srinivasa (Padmaja), Freelance journalist from India possesses Bachelor degree in Engineering (B.E) and Post graduate in Business Management (MBA) with Distinction. He has worked as Associate Editor of 'Naradar' fortnightly journal in Chennai, India. He is the Senior Editor of the journal "The Divineness".

He has contributed articles, short stories and travelogues in leading journals like Ananda Vikatan, Kumudam, Savi, Kalki, Dinamani Kadhir, Dinamani daily, Idhayam Pesukirathu and Naradar etc

He has written articles and e books through Smashwords Inc, Kindle Direct Publishing, Atlanta publications, Cooperjal publications (UK) and lulu.com. His contributions are seen in ezinearticles.com, shvoong.com, iproclaim.com

(USA) and TCC news (Germany).He is the Consulting Editor: Contemporary Who's Who-Research Board of Advisers of ABI, USA.

View his books

https://www.amazon.com/-/e/B01G3JTQ92

Dedicated to My Dear Parents

Preface

A care for the industrial welfare is a 'must'.

Overlooking the genuineness of their demands regarding sufferings will only make the work force rise with anger.

If they are understandable, then the problem is eliminated. So, a good reasoning power, healthy approach is essential for managing Conflicts and Collective bargaining!

Total submission to the unions is also inadmissible. The management should always be in the elated state at the same time show consideration without total submission.

Contents

Conflict

"Conflict is an unavoidable devil"- says a leading Industrialist

'Business World' had published the above version in one of its issues.

"Strike does not worry me but the hunger and sufferings which the worker's family forced to face worries me!"- C.E.O of Birla Group, when a severe strike caused closure of its group of companies.

Strike is the results of conflicts.

Hence it has to be dealt with other ill-happenings like lockouts, violence, ghero etc which also result due to conflict.

Managing Conflicts

"Breathe in wisdom and breathe out confront" said a CEO of a MNC.

Like a cat and rat, the rubbing of shoulders will only create confusion and calamity. A placid look on matters will fetch better harmony while managing conflicts.

A care for the industrial welfare is a 'must'.

Overlooking the genuineness of their demands regarding sufferings will only make the work force rise with anger.

If they are understandable, then the problem is eliminated.

So, a good reasoning power and healthy approach is essential for managing conflict.

Total submission to the unions is also inadmissible.

The management should always be in the elated state at the same time show consideration without total submission.

'Nip it in the bud' policy is always favorable.

Instead of having talents to face the conflicts, the management should possess the shrewdness to avert all conflicts in the early stages itself.

If it succeeds in it, then the whole process of industrial dispute and vehemence will be eradicated.

Expectations of the work force should be foresighted by the management and act accordingly.
The inner desire of an individual is that he requires recognition and sympathy to his feelings and setbacks.

If he is found neglected then he becomes violent to establish his foothold.

'Come what may' attitude will lead to rupture.

'Give and take' policy will always play a safe role.

Bargaining in the right spirit to pacify the work force is essential.

'Offering cash in suit case' policy will not thrive for a long period.

In many industries union leaders are 'purchased' for establishing industrial peace.

If the weaknesses of the union are utilized, then the management can combat conflict in a cunning way and deceit the poor work force.

Two way traffic exchanges of views should exist.

Total domination of the management will create an unhealthy atmosphere. To make the situation conducive, a patient hearing is essential for amicable solution.

Some management follows the 'Split and rule policy'.

Amongst the unions a sense of misunderstanding and break are created and this will result an easy way of tackling the situation for the management.

Hence the unions, work force always give out slogans saying 'Long live unity'.

Because a split will cause a set of work force to report for duty while others will abstain from duty. As the management will manage to run the show with these work forces, the strike will become a 'flop'.

Event in a leading MNC

Several years back a leading private MNC faced a severe setback when Engineers Association went for a strike to get its demands.

But the demands were vehemently refused by the management.

Power production was nil.

Grid condition became poor affecting all industries in South India.

Ministry for Energy and Power was pressurizing from Delhi.

Situation became critical when the strike extended for weeks together.

Police forces were deputed and Engineers were chased and dragged to the plant.

At that time management took a wise decision to 'split and rule'.

There was only one association for Engineers, containing Diploma and Degree holders.

The clever management mooted an ideal trick stating that Graduate Engineers will be specially treated if they come out with a separate union or association.

This created a break.

A big bang was there to start a Graduate Engineers Association.

Engineers Association was split into two and three Graduates were offered lucrative amenities, perks in contrast to the fellow diploma holders, which made the Graduate Engineers to enter the plant and start the machines for power generation!!A big mammoth conflict was broken to pieces by the management and gradually knowing their weakness, the striking engineers complied with the management's orders.

Clever Administrator

It happened in the office a popular Tamil weekly journal.

The CEO/Proprietor of that journal was a very clever administrator. All the employees had faith and respect for him. Loyalty was cent percent and that journal thrived in all aspects.

Due to age, the CEO handed over the responsibilities to his son and made him as CEO.

At the time of takeover by the son of that CEO, many senior journalists were working in that organization.

A regular conflict was there between the new CEO and the senior journalists.

While meetings were conducted for writing editorials, clash of old thoughts and new concepts were there.

Bubbling with energy the young CEO could not face the senior experienced personalities as their knowledge and depth of experience were too high.

So, conflicts fired up!

The matter was appraised to his father and ex CEO/Proprietor.

One fine day, the salary of all senior journalists in that journal was shot up exorbitantly and so too in the Film Studios owned by that management.

All were bewildered and could not guess why such a huge remuneration all of a sudden.

It was the clever knack played by Ex CEO /Proprietor.

When an employee, who was very close to that CEO, asked the reason for this dramatic change, smilingly the Proprietor replied "Light, which is going to be put out, will glow tremendously".

Next month along with the pay cover a letter of dismissal of all senior journalists and staff was issued.

To satisfy his son and to save the day to day conflicts arising in that journal, which affected its coverage of news as per the wishes of his son, ex CEO handled it in this fashion.

Event in a Film Studios

A senior hero was engaged in a film, shot by a clever producer.

Being a talented producer, he used to handle the actors in a businesslike manner.

Glorifying them too much is not his policy.

Whatever respects he demanded from them, had to be given to him.

If they fail, he reacted sharply and cunningly.

That hero's attitude and others engaged in the production turned out to be intolerable.

Hero started dictating terms and induced others in the organization too, in a high handed fashion, for 'more pay'.

Knowing well his weaknesses, the producer planned to end this conflict, which had poisoned his organization and retarded the production of the film and morality and self respect.

Next day shooting was fighting scene for hero with swords with villain.

Instead of an ordinary artiste he appointed a talented fighter for villain's role with real might and with all coolness handed over real original swords (well sharpened) to both, instead of wooden or paper swords which are usually used!!

Immediately knowing the severe danger behind this, the Hero was dumb founded and stunned!

But the producer cunningly remarked "No problem!"
You are no doubt a Hero! I admit it! Also, I admit your huge demands to be right and reasonable! As per the screen play you have to win over the villain. Let me see how you do it. Let your fans also see it. Hence this special arrangement! You reveal your mettle now with the real sword instead of wooden fake sword! I shall pay you the desired amount you demand!"

The trembled Hero totally surrendered, breaking the conflict which was created by him and his supporters in the popular Film Studios, talking ill of that producer's conflict management style.

The above example may look simple, but the presence of mind of the administrator to tackle the conflict is also important.

An air of protest and conflict was spreading in the entire organization, as the Hero created an impression that not only he, but all were paid less than what they deserve!

So, with all intelligence the producer, who is an able administrator, took this drastic step to collapse the conflict!

Collective Bargaining

A negotiation between representatives of employers and workers to determine conditions of labor is a development of the Industrial Revolution.

Matters pertaining to Collective Bargaining in a PSU:

-recruitment

-retrenchment

-retirement

-promotion

-minimum wage

-working condition

-disciplinary actions, methods

-allowances

-special amenities

Process:

-The management will have to be flexible and so also the workers.

-Both parties should not be adamant in 'giving' and 'taking' terms.

-Aiming amicable solution rather than confusion and calamity.

-Maintaining their stands in a cordial manner.

Stages of Agreements:

-Negotiations

-Implementation

-Revisions

Its success is due to the moral strength rather than the legal force of agreements.

During the past several years legislation has been passed to facilitate the peaceful settlement of industrial disputes between employers and Unions.

Some recommendations were made later as follows:

Joint industrial councils are set up in well organized industry.

Works committees representatives of management and workers be set up in individual establishments and meet regularly on an equal footing to consider matters of mutual interest in the daily life of workers.

In 1971 the Industrial Relations Act was established and in 1972 contracts of Employment Act.
So, in these stages an aim for amicable settlement was perceived by the management and labor force.

Based on the above developments, Collective Bargaining takes place with all good motives in that PSU.

Negotiations:

An agreement is arrived at after peaceful negotiations.

With a friendly motive and without prejudice all the terms will be spoken.

Give and take policy holds the key.

They sign an agreement, which becomes a Contract.

Implementation:

The methods in which the terms to be implemented will be mentioned and any dubious aspects of it are analyzed and resolved.

Revision:

The date of expiry of the terms and condition concluded will be mentioned specifically. Then only the next discussion will be conducted after the expiry period mentioned.

So, implementation and revision of collectively bargained terms and provisions is a continuous phenomenon.

Follow up and necessary analysis of the agreements, are done with care.

Preparatory Stages

Before taking up negotiations the 7 unions underwent following preparatory stages:

Unions' Move for Negotiations

-Arising of Problem

-Feasibility Report

-Comparing with similar industry with existing conditions

-Consult workers in site

-New demands or changes

-Grievance study

-Economic information

-Clear cut demands

-Communication to all members

-Advice to members for cooperation and peace

-Facing the Collective Bargaining Scene

Employers' Move:

-Arise Of Problems

-Anticipation of Demands

-Comparison with other similar Units

-Analysis of Grievances

-Conduct Meetings

-Exchange of views with other Companies

-Study Labor Law Provisions

-Economic ability of the Company

-Labor Relation Study

-Tentative Decisions

-Negotiator Selection

Facing the Collective Bargaining Scene

As mentioned above the employee and the employer prepare themselves for Collective Bargaining in that PSU.

By studying the implications and financial capacity of the organization the union can judge what to ask.

Also by studying the neighboring companies they can compare and demand.

Discussion with staff actually facing the problems will help them to speak well in the bargaining.

Advising members to be calm gives an assured healthy climate of understanding harmony and peace.

So, in the case of employers, before going for collective bargaining should be prepared with anticipation of demands, examine labor relations policy and know the economic conditions of the company's commitments.

A good negotiator is a 'must' and full trust is placed on his gentleness, ability and tactfulness.

In our organization Chief General Manager (Personnel) is appointed as Negotiator with General Manager (P&A), Unit heads and Labor Welfare Officer to assist.

Tacts Followed:

-Listening calmly

-Questioning the evidence offered

-Using verified data

-Patiently looking one matter after another

-Not threatening violence

-To cut down emotional feelings

-To jump to another subject decently if ambiguity arises with ugly arguments.

-To consider monetary agreement

-Maintaining goodwill and coordination.

All care is taken to draft an agreement since it has to exist for a particular period and between that periods no claims can be made.

Points to be noted before Drafting

-Clear and easily understandable

-Legal terms and technical terms precise

-No omissions and no ambiguity

-Superfluous adjectives and adverbs beating the bush phrases are avoided.

Contents of the Draft:

-Names of the representatives of parties, their designations and the organizations to which they belong to.

-Reference of all demands irrespective of whether they have been dropped withdrawn on cancelled.

-Duration of operations.

-Dates of implementations

-Provisions abiding with law.

In this manner collective bargaining is implemented in our organization

Incident 1 in a PSU:

At the main gate of the factory the security force demanded identification card from an individual entering the entrance for duty.

But the worker expressed that he did not have one.

The security spoke in Hindi in an abusing way and prevented him from entering.

The worker protested vehemently to go in as there will be loss of pay for them.

A tussle broke out and the security force opened fire against the group of workers, who raised a protest against his demand of identity card.

Such incidents usually happen in other units too.

Hence the Joint Council of Unions protested and underwent a strike, a flash strike (100% illegal).

What the Unions felt was that such armed force should be posted not at the entrance since many thousands of contract labor forces in that factory, which are yet to be regularized, are already posted at the entrance as security to check.

"The private security forces are from outside regions and also they are with weapons.

Only in theft prone areas the security forces with weapons should be posted and also a known person from the unit should be posted at the gate of each unit for quick identification in the absence of identification card".

Above version was the demand of the unions.

The individual was actually not issued identification card, since new entrants are given only after 6 months.

Without knowing this status, a rupture has been created by wounding of 28 persons, looting of shops, ransacking nearby shops etc.

An agreement was signed and the security forces were posted in the areas mentioned by the Unions and suitable alternative staffs were appointed at the gate for identification. A separate register was maintained and names of the person entering without identity and names of the witness for him to enter were recorded.

In all the units this has been implemented and Collective Bargaining for employment of casual laborers, contract laborers, safety of the work force, cordial understanding with security and workmen were resulted.

Incident 2 in a PSU

The persons employed in a hazardous division did not enjoy any benefits compared to persons working in less hazardous areas.

By working in most health hazardous areas, lots of energy will be extracted from an individual, apart from high risk.

Exposed to hot conditions all the 24 hours is not an easy task.

Hence the Labor Unions demanded special pay, allowances, promotion benefits etc for persons working there.

For this

\-The financial commitments were studied first.

-Actual hardships faced by those workers were consulted and discussed.

-For promotions and allowances, bargaining was done according to the hazards faced.

-Betterment of wages for those persons, all data regarding fatal accidents, injuries, and unsafe practices were discussed.

-Special seniority for house allotment, promotion, foreign training was demanded scrupulously.

-Liberal emoluments and facilities were chalked out after studying the conditions of those risky work spots.

-All those staffs were requested to be calm until the negotiations were completed.

-Interim relief was obtained (in few thousands of rupees) to pacify these people.

-The management too was very tactful and prevented any untoward incident to happen.

-Economic stability was assured and then a special wage scale with special hazardous allowance, shift allowance, depth allowance, dust allowance, risk allowance etc was sanctioned.

-Houses near the work spot area were allotted only to these people for them to attend duty without much strain.

A labor relation was studied well and as a negotiator the Director of the organization was posted to handle it smoothly.

Along with him, the Deputy General Manager (Safety) and Deputy General Manager (Operations) were appointed.

Due to this Collective Bargaining, both the Unions and the management had good mutual trust and understanding.

That PSU has bagged the award for best cordial industrial relationship year after year.

This is a solid example for outstanding Collective Bargaining with tact and gentleness.

View other books from Chakrapani Srinivasa

Strange India

https://www.amazon.co.uk/dp/B07S73LCTK

Kohlinoor of India: Winner Virat Kohli

https://www.amazon.co.uk/dp/B07SKNRVCT

Never Forgotten Naradar Srinivasa Rao: Most Enterprising Journalist

https://www.amazon.co.uk/dp/B07NLFY73C

How to Manage Funds in an Organization?

https://www.amazon.co.uk/dp/B00Z0Q8IF8

Wonders of Nano Technology

https://www.amazon.co.uk/dp/B07D3ZP7MC

https://www.amazon.com/dp/B08BF4HCVX

What are the Best HRD Tactics?

https://www.amazon.co.uk/dp/B07HZ7JK18

Solar Energy Plans in Tamilnadu

https://www.amazon.co.uk/dp/B01G44ZL4K

How to Forecast Manpower Needs in an Organization: You Have The Skill!

https://www.amazon.co.uk/dp/B0111GBZKK

Infrastructure in India

https://www.amazon.co.uk/dp/B0163777RW

Accountant's Role in an Organization: A book for Accountants

https://www.amazon.co.uk/dp/B00YYHDHU0

Inland Waterways and Hydro Power in India

https://www.amazon.co.uk/dp/B015NEZMXW

Conflict Management Styles and Collective Bargaining

https://www.amazon.co.uk/dp/B00Z3B9GTW

Quiz and General Knowledge

https://www.amazon.co.uk/dp/B01N4M99S7

In Search of Paradise and Peace

https://www.amazon.co.uk/dp/B07C7F3XKM

Graphene -The God of Nano Technology

https://www.amazon.co.uk/dp/B07561LWTT

You Can Gain Power and Authority

https://www.amazon.co.uk/dp/B00YWY9QR8

HRD Systems and Management by
Objectives

https://www.amazon.co.uk/dp/B016UC9UKC

International Conferences on Nanotechnology
in India

https://www.amazon.co.uk/dp/B07BP8YLJZ

Holy Madhwa Saints: Get Divine Pleasure by Reading

https://www.amazon.co.uk/dp/B010WNBYU4

Trade Shows in India and Participants

https://www.amazon.co.uk/dp/B016PV1KS8

Collaboration and Intervention Techniques

https://www.amazon.co.uk/dp/B0110DLE8C

How to Plan Career and Quality Discipline in an Organization? Plan for Prosperity

https://www.amazon.co.uk/dp/B011GXOXIE

How to Speak Skillfully?

https://www.amazon.com/dp/B08BJ8PCKT

How to Supervise Efficiently?

https://www.amazon.com/dp/B08BNFYSPQ- e book

How to Develop Systems for Profit?

https://www.amazon.com/dp/B08BYVL2P9

Nanotechnology Research in India

https://www.amazon.com/dp/B08BZDFVR8

How to Create a Turnaround in Your Organization?

https://www.amazon.com/dp/B08C97X2F9?ref_=pe_3052080_397514860

What are the Best Strategies for Your Company to Grow?

https://www.amazon.com/dp/B08CC8Z9F9

How to Plan and Control Successfully?

https://www.amazon.com/dp/B08CRSTW38

How to become a talented Manager?

https://www.amazon.com/dp/B08DNWKLL2

How to Win the Grace of God?

https://www.amazon.com/dp/B08DL1LMTZ

Tutorial and Hand book for Accountants

https://www.amazon.com/dp/B08DVCHNX9

Jokes & Satire

https://www.amazon.com/dp/B08DYB73Z3

Click to see my e books published by Amazon

https://www.amazon.com/-/e/B01G3JTQ92